For Clark & Mary,
Two very special friends
Christmas 1987
from
Billy & Bunby,
with love.
xxx

WESTERN WILDLIFE

WESTERN WILDLIFE

By Dennis and Esther Schmidt

Esther Schmidt

Dennis Schmidt

Toronto
OXFORD UNIVERSITY PRESS
1983

This book is dedicated to
the cause of wildlife conservation.

ACKNOWLEDGEMENTS

We are grateful to Michael Beery, John Edwards,
Ernie Kuyt, Ray Lord, Gordon Rowe, and Roger Boulton
for their assistance and co-operation.

CANADIAN CATALOGUING IN PUBLICATION DATA
Schmidt, Dennis, 1921-
    Western wildlife

Bibliography: p.
Includes index.
ISBN 0-19-540415-7

1. Mammals — Canada, Western. 2. Birds — Canada,
Western. 3. Reptiles — Canada, Western. 4. Insects —
Canada, Western. I. Schmidt, Esther, 1922-
II. Title.

QL221.W47S35   591.9712   C82-095197-8

© Oxford University Press (Canadian Branch) 1983
OXFORD is a trademark of Oxford University Press.
ISBN 0-19-540415-7
1 2 3 4 — 6 5 4 3
Designed by Heather Smith Delfino
Printed in Hong Kong by
EVERBEST PRINTING COMPANY LIMITED

INTRODUCTION

The photographs displayed in this book can only hint at the joy we have experienced over the years, travelling western Canada and getting to know the land and its wildlife. We make no claim to be scientists. Neither zoologists, nor ornithologists, nor entomologists, we are simply photographers who are possessed with a love of the wild.

Growing up nearly half a century ago, Dennis on a farm in Saskatchewan and Esther on Vancouver Island, we had the good fortune to develop our love of both nature and photography at an early age. Esther was given her first Kodak Box Brownie when she was eight, and Dennis graduated from a borrowed box camera to his own at the age of sixteen.

We met each other, appropriately enough, at an amateur camera club in 1968, and later married. When, in the seventies, we retired, we couldn't stand the thought of spending the rest of our lives idle, so we decided to devote ourselves to photography. We now live in the town of Kimberley, up in the Kootenay Mountains, where, less than three miles from home, we can be out in the wild among the animals. After a lifetime of engineering and office work, it's a marvellous feeling of freedom to be alone with nature.

Although we can claim to have photographed most of the wild species of western Canada, we cannot possibly put them all in one book. Still less can we hope to portray all our experiences — far more precious to us than the pictures they yielded — with animals such as the coyote that showed its goodwill to us by gently taking Esther's hands into its jaws and releasing them without a mark, or the hummingbird that hovered still while we stroked its chin. Once when Dennis was filming coyotes tracking bighorn sheep, a wolf sat only a few feet behind him, quietly watching the show. Another time, the leader of a wapiti herd came out of the forest up to Esther, licked her cheek, and turned back to lead its group across the clearing. We have seen a wolverine rear up on its hind legs as we approached and stand shading its eyes from the sun with a paw, the better to watch our every move.

Once assured that we meant no harm, the animals have always seemed to accept us as friends. On the other hand, trespassing on an animal's territory has occasionally earned us a well-deserved reprisal — as when a white-tailed buck drove Dennis up a tree and kept him there for hours, raking down all the lower branches with its antlers and hoofs. Yet wherever we have been, among bears, moose, wapiti, cougars, or wolves, we have never carried a weapon — and never will. We have found that, entrusting ourselves to nature, we are trusted in turn.

One evening, when the foot of a rainbow crossed between two grazing pronghorns above us, it was as if the spirit that moves in all things stood on the hillside. Indeed, we believe that our experiences with our fellow inhabitants of the Canadian wild have been a gracious gift to us. It is in the hope of sharing our joys with others that we have undertaken this book.

Kimberley, B.C.   DENNIS and ESTHER SCHMIDT
January 1983

CAPTIONS

7

Migrating long-billed dowitchers rest and feed at the Fraser River Delta before resuming their flight south. They are accompanied by a spotted redshank, a rare visitor native to northern Scandinavia and eastern Siberia.

8-9

Breeding pairs of bald eagles occupy the same nest year after year, adding more material every season. The young will continue to use the huge structure as a resting platform for some time after they are fledged.

10

Clark's nutcrackers are year-round residents of the Rockies. Related to the common crow, they are equipped with expandable cheek pouches which allow them to transport quantities of conifer seeds for storage.

11

The great horned owl spends most of the daylight hours asleep. At night it uses its powerful eyes, silent wings, and formidable talons to hunt a wide range of prey, including grouse, crows, and rabbits. Smaller animals are swallowed whole.

12

Roughly 100 metres from shore, these red-necked grebes were photographed by radio remote control; the camera was encased in a special underwater housing and anchored about one metre from the nest.

1

The purple sea-star is only one of approximately ninety species of starfish found along the coast of British Columbia. It preys on the mussels and barnacles of the middle and upper tidal zones.

2-3

As their name suggests, harbour seals favour the protected waters close to shore — these two were photographed in Barclay Sound, on the west coast of Vancouver Island. Though basically coastal animals, they may travel as much as eighty kilometres upriver, especially when the salmon are spawning.

4-5

Nomadic killer whales are attracted to the abundant fish and squid along the Pacific coast. Like all whales, they can remain underwater for long periods but must surface to breathe; used air is expelled and fresh taken in through the nostril, or blow-hole, on top of the head.

6

A great blue heron stalks the shoreline in search of fish and water snakes. Despite its size — the 'great blue' is the largest heron in North America — it usually nests in tree-top colonies.

1 PURPLE SEA-STAR

2 HARBOUR SEAL

4 KILLER WHALE

6 GREAT BLUE HERON

7   LONG-BILLED DOWITCHERS

8 BALD EAGLE

9 BALD EAGLE

11 GREAT HORNED OWL

12 RED-NECKED GREBES

CAPTIONS

13

A large, powerful, and intelligent weasel, the wolverine is capable of bringing down a moose. For the most part, however, it subsists on the remains of kills made by other predators. Any leftovers are marked with a strong musky odour and cached away for future use.

14-16

The highest peaks of British Columbia, Alberta, the Yukon, and Alaska are home to the mountain goat — even in winter. Its narrow build allows safe passage along the treacherous ledges, while its hoofs are specially adapted to provide traction on the ice.

17-20

In summer bighorn sheep roam the cliffs and meadows of the high Rockies, but winter forces them to retreat to lower elevations where the vegetation is less deeply buried in snow. Spending most of the year in bachelor groups, mature rams often stage mild butting displays to establish rank; however, really serious battles rarely occur outside of the mating season.

21-2

Dall's sheep rest in the snow to chew the cud. Ranging from northern British Columbia into the Yukon and Alaska, this species closely resembles its more southerly relative, the bighorn, in many of its social habits.

23-4

The Shawnee name *wapiti* refers to the pale rump patch of this magnificent deer (also known as the American elk). The six-pointed antlers of a mature male may measure more than a metre and a half across.

13 WOLVERINE

15 MOUNTAIN GOATS

16 MOUNTAIN GOAT

18 BIGHORN SHEEP

19 BIGHORN SHEEP

23 WAPITI

24 WAPITI

CAPTIONS

25-7

When the autumn rut is over, bull wapiti leave their harems and form bachelor groups; cows and calves spend the winter together in herds of up to a hundred.

28

A bull moose stands nearly knee-deep in November snow. His massive antlers will drop by mid-winter; starting to grow again in the spring, they will reach full size in time for the mating season.

29

Puma, panther, catamount, mountain lion, or cougar — this expert deer-hunter is known by many names. In Canada, its range is now almost entirely restricted to British Columbia and western Alberta.

30

Late September finds the white-tailed ptarmigan about halfway through its autumn moult; when the change is complete, it will be pure white. A summer resident of the high alpine regions of British Columbia and western Alberta, it descends to lower elevations for the winter.

31

Large ears alert for danger, a mule deer doe and her fawn browse on their winter feed of tender evergreen twigs. The fawn, which will stay with its mother until spring, may be ready to breed itself by the fall.

32

The coyote may be most closely associated with the prairies, but its range extends almost throughout North America. This animal was photographed in the mountainous Bow Valley region of Alberta.

33

The story-books have been unfair to the wolf. In fact, it kills only as much as it needs to feed itself and its family. The male brings food to his mate while she is nursing. Later both parents supply the pups with partially digested meat.

34

Long legs and oversized feet enable the lynx to keep up with its favourite food — the snowshoe hare. Records show that lynx numbers vary with the hare's population cycle, which peaks about every ten years.

35

The American kestrel, or sparrow hawk, is common throughout southern Canada. Here, its nesting site is a clay bank in British Columbia's Okanagan Valley. Since it feeds mainly on pests such as mice and grasshoppers, this species is a valuable predator in agricultural areas.

36

The blue grouse, one of Canada's largest, inhabits subalpine wood burns and forest clearings. This female has chosen a high perch to watch over her chicks as they feed in the grass below.

27   WAPITI

31 MULE DEER

33 WOLF

35 AMERICAN KESTREL

36 BLUE GROUSE

CAPTIONS

37

Wings beating fifty-five times a second, a female rufous hummingbird hovers over her two bean-sized eggs. The narrow opening of the bowl-shaped nest is designed to prevent heat loss. This species spends the summer in British Columbia and winters in Mexico.

38

Yellow-bellied marmots dig their burrows in the rock piles and talus slopes east of the Cascade Mountains. Living in large colonies, they have developed a highly effective way of guarding against intruders: at the slightest hint of danger, a sentry stationed high on a rocky outcrop alerts the entire community.

39

Nicknamed the 'whistler', the hoary marmot too uses the sentry system to protect members of the colony when they are out foraging. Its habitat is the remote alpine tundra of the Rockies (above tree-line), north into the Yukon.

40

The arid valleys of south-central British Columbia are home to the Pacific rattlesnake. Like other members of its family, it injects its prey (frogs, birds, and small rodents) with venom and swallows it whole. It adds another hollow segment to its warning 'rattle' every time it sheds its skin.

41

Shown here surrounded by the swamp laurel and sphagnum moss of an alpine meadow, the western toad is found in moist habitats throughout the west. Its warts — which are not contagious — secrete an irritant that discourages predators.

42-3

The cinnamon colour phase is not uncommon among black bears. A true omnivore, the bruin eats greens as well as honey, fruit, insects, small mammals, and carrion.

44

The Columbian ground squirrel lives in colonies in the mountain meadows and valleys of southern British Columbia and Alberta. Unlike many rodents, it occasionally eats insects and carrion in addition to plant material.

45

Approximately 30,000 barbed quills protect all but the face and underside of the porcupine. An expert climber, it feeds on the leaves, twigs, buds, and inner bark of both deciduous and coniferous trees.

46

A male mountain bluebird feeds insects to a nestful of hungry young. More colourful than the female, he shares feeding duties with her. The nesting cavity is an old woodpecker hole.

47

Beautiful, bold, and noisy, the Steller's jay is a common sight in the forests of British Columbia. Although insects, fruit, and nuts are the staples of its diet, it is not above taking other birds' eggs as a supplement.

48

The Polyphemus moth is found in semi-arid regions across North America. Once the sensational wings develop, the adult insect does not eat but subsists on food stored during the caterpillar stage.

38 YELLOW-BELLIED MARMOTS

39 HOARY MARMOTS

40 PACIFIC RATTLESNAKE

42 BLACK BEAR

44 COLUMBIAN GROUND SQUIRREL

45 PORCUPINE

46 MOUNTAIN BLUEBIRD

47 STELLER'S JAY

48 POLYPHEMUS MOTH

CAPTIONS

49

Barely eighteen centimetres long (about the size of a bluebird), the tiny pygmy owl feeds mainly on mice, voles, and small birds. Unlike most members of the owl family, it is often active during the day.

50

The Rocky Mountain pika, a small cousin of the rabbits and hares, is found on boulder-strewn slopes from the Rockies west to the coast. Since it does not hibernate, it must spend much of the summer gathering, drying, and storing vegetation for the winter.

51

The osprey's powerful feet are specially adapted for catching and carrying fish. Back at the nest, the male eats the head and offers the rest of the fish to the female, who feeds the more tender parts to the young.

52

The long-legged moose is ideally built for wading. Aquatic plants such as pondweeds make up a good portion of its summer diet.

53

A superb swimmer, the common loon rarely comes ashore except to nest — its legs are set so far back on its body that land travel is difficult. Here, a female tends the nest while her mate dives for food.

54-5

The wild turkey is the ancestor of our table bird; first domesticated by the Aztecs, it was taken to Europe by the Spanish conquistadores. The native species had disappeared from Canada by the beginning of this century, but it is now being introduced in areas such as British Columbia's Kootenays.

56

A Coeur d'Alene salamander makes a rare appearance in the sunlight: because its skin requires constant moisture, it spends most of its time under cover of the leaves, moss, and rotting wood on the forest floor. This species is native to southeastern British Columbia.

57

The common garter snake is widespread throughout North America. A non-venomous species, it is harmless to all but the insects, slugs, and frogs on which it feeds.

58

This cow moose will take devoted care of her calf throughout the coming winter; nevertheless, she will have to drive it away to fend for itself before her next calf is born.

59-60

The mule deer is at home throughout the west, from the open forests of the Rockies to the sagebrush coulees of the prairies. The nickname 'jumping deer' refers to its distinctive reaction when surprised or threatened.

49 PYGMY OWL

52 MOOSE

55 WILD TURKEY

57 COMMON GARTER SNAKES

CAPTIONS

61

A fledgling prairie falcon exercises its long narrow wings in preparation for the first flight. With practice, it will reach a cruising speed of fifty kilometres per hour; when it spots a likely catch (rodent, bird, or insect) it will attack in a dive that may exceed 300 kilometres per hour.

62

Shortly after birth, a white-tailed deer tends to her wobbly-legged fawn. Slightly smaller than the mule deer, the white-tail ranges across most of southern Canada.

63

A robin-sized predator, the loggerhead shrike has the beak of a hawk but the delicate feet of a songbird. Because it is unable to hold its prey in the usual manner while it feeds, it impales its catch (a mouse or small bird) on a thorn or spike of barbed wire.

64-5

The red fox has often been accused of stealing chickens, but in fact it is more likely to assist the farmer by controlling pests: insects and small mammals such as mice are the mainstays of its diet.

66

A beaver adds another stick to its carefully-constructed dam. By creating a pond deep enough that it will not freeze to the bottom, the dam will ensure the beaver's access to its underwater food cache in the winter.

67

The familiar rabbit of the plains, Nuttall's cottontail upholds the family reputation for breeding. Once sexual maturity is reached — at the age of three months — a female can produce as many as four litters of five or six young each in a single season.

68

The red-necked grebe, like the loon, is an expert diver — more at home in the water than on land. Male and female take turns incubating the eggs, which are laid on a floating pyramid of vegetation anchored to the bottom by reeds.

69

Every fall, vast flocks of snow geese pass through the central prairies en route from their Arctic breeding grounds to wintering areas in the southern United States. Other flocks use the Pacific flyway and spend the winter on the salt marshes and fields of the Pacific coast.

70-1

Isolated inland lakes are the summer home of the white pelican. The feeding behaviour of this species is highly sociable: sometimes a group of up to twelve birds will fish together, forming a circle and dipping their huge bills in unison to catch the fish trapped in the middle.

72

The yellow-headed blackbird is a colonial species found in wetlands across the west, from British Columbia to the Ontario border. Its nest is constructed of water-soaked vegetation woven to growing plants; as the wet material dries, it shrinks, attaching the structure firmly to its supports.

63 LOGGERHEAD SHRIKE

65   RED FOX

66 BEAVER

69 SNOW GEESE

70 WHITE PELICAN

72 YELLOW-HEADED BLACKBIRD

CAPTIONS

73

Avocets often feed in groups of fifty or more. Wading side by side in the shallows of a lake or slough, they use their gracefully up-curved bills to scythe through the water in search of insect larvae and crustaceans.

74

Migrating Canada geese rest and wait for the ice to melt before resuming their flight to the low Arctic breeding grounds. Family bonds in this species are extremely strong: pairs mate for life, and the young stay with their parents throughout their first year.

75

The Arctic fox may be forced to travel far outside its normal home range when its staple food — the lemming — is in short supply. Sightings in Manitoba have been reported as far south as the 51st parallel.

76-7

Accustomed to diving for its food (aquatic plants make up the bulk of its diet), the muskrat builds its lodge with an underwater entrance. Inside is a comfortable nesting platform, well above the water level.

78

The killdeer is a common inland shorebird. Probably best-known for its 'broken-wing' act, it runs or flies about erratically whenever its territory is disturbed, to distract attention from the nest. The species' name is derived from its frantic distress call.

79-81

The pronghorn — the fastest mammal in North America — ranges throughout the Great Plains Basin. In a sense, it is a prehistoric relic: the only remaining member of a family midway between the antlered deer and the horned animals such as sheep and goats. Unlike any other horned animal, it sheds the outer shells of its permanent horns every year, as if they were antlers.

82

A male horned lark feeds his hungry chick. A ground-nesting species, this bird is perfectly at home on the treeless prairie. The curving black 'horns' on either side of its head are erectile feathers.

83

Burrowing animals such as ground squirrels, gophers, and prairie dogs stand little chance against the badger. The long claws on its powerful front feet enable it to outdig any prey with ease.

84

Even in winter, the river otter spends most of its time in the water. Diving for its food (mainly fish) through a hole in the ice, it can remain submerged for four minutes or more.

73 AVOCETS

74 CANADA GEESE

75 ARCTIC FOX

77 MUSKRAT

78 KILLDEER

81 PRONGHORNS

84 RIVER OTTER

CAPTIONS

85

The western meadowlark makes its presence known from before dawn till well after sunset with its cheerful, melodious song. Though related to the blackbird, it is coloured to blend into its open field habitat.

86

The marbled godwit is most often seen probing mudflats or lakeshores for worms and crustaceans. For nesting and rearing its young, however, this large shore-bird prefers a grassy meadow.

87

Only about twenty-three centimetres long, the burrowing owl makes its home in an abandoned badger or prairie-dog hole. Young birds deter any intruders by imitating a rattlesnake's warning buzz.

88-9

Black-tailed prairie dogs are now found in only a handful of colonies in southern Saskatchewan and the western United States. A town may cover sixty hectares or more, and is divided into distinct sections. The characteristic greeting 'kiss' allows neighbours to recognize one another.

90

In late autumn, two bison graze on the prairie where once vast herds of their ancestors roamed. Hunted nearly to extinction by 1900, the North American buffalo now survives in only a few protected areas.

91

Equipped with long back legs and a powerful tail, the Ord's kangaroo rat can hop up to two metres in a single bound. It gets all the moisture it needs from its food, and can survive without drinking water.

92

A Richardson's ground squirrel — better known, perhaps, as a gopher — gathers nesting material. Its voracious appetite for seeds and tender greens makes this species a constant problem for grain farmers.

93

Most often seen darting through the evening sky in search of insects, the common nighthawk spends the daylight hours resting. The lengthwise perching posture not only provides camouflage, but helps the short-legged bird to balance on the branch.

94

The coyote has often been unjustly blamed for killing livestock. In fact, it finds a good deal of its food as carrion; its hunting is generally limited to smaller prey such as mice and rabbits.

95

Twice a year, almost the entire world population of whooping cranes passes through Saskatchewan on migration. In 1937 only fifteen of these magnificent birds survived; by 1982 an intensive campaign of research and public education had helped their numbers to increase to eighty.

96

A ferruginous hawk soars through the clear prairie sky as it scans the ground far below for food. This beautiful predator is now becoming rare in many parts of its range.

85   WESTERN MEADOWLARK

86 MARBLED GODWIT

87 BURROWING OWL

90 BISON

92 RICHARDSON'S GROUND SQUIRREL

93 COMMON NIGHTHAWK

95 WHOOPING CRANES

96 FERRUGINOUS HAWK

INDEX OF PLATES

___

SELECTED REFERENCES

___

Banfield, A.W.F. *The Mammals of Canada*. Toronto: University of Toronto Press, 1974.

Borror, D.J., and R.E. White. *A Field Guide to the Insects of America North of Mexico*. Boston: Houghton Mifflin Co., 1970.

Burt, W.H. *A Field Guide to the Mammals*. Third ed. Boston: Houghton Mifflin Co., 1976.

Dalton, S. *Borne on the Wind: The Extraordinary World of Insects*. New York: Reader's Digest Press, 1975.

Geist, V. 'Mountain Goat Behavior'. *Wildlife Review*, Summer 1971.

Godfrey, W.E. *The Birds of Canada*. National Museums of Canada Bulletin 203, 1966.

Goodwin, G., *et al. The Animal Kingdom*. Three vols. F. Drimmer, ed.-in-chief. New York: Greystone Press, 1954.

Kool, R. 'Edges'. *Wildlife Review*, Winter 1981.

Larousse Encyclopedia of the Animal World. P.P. Grasse, ed. New York: Larousse & Co., Inc. 1975.

Nowak, R., *et al. Wild Animals of North America*. T.B. Allen, ed. Washington, D.C.: National Geographic Society, 1979.

Peterson, R.T. *A Field Guide to Western Birds*. Boston: Houghton Mifflin Co., 1972.

Savage, A. and C. *Wild Mammals of Western Canada*. Saskatoon, Sask.: Western Producer Prairie Books, 1981.

___